Melinda's Bee-Hive

A series of eight poems in 2 volumes about the life of a worker honey bee, called Melinda.

Author's acknowledgements
In memory of my father.

First edition 2014. Published by Northern Bee Books
Published by Northern Bee Books
Scout Bottom Farm
Mytholmroyd
Hebden Bridge HX7 5JS (UK)
Volume 1 ISBN 978-1-908904-66-9
Volume 2 ISBN 978-1-908904-67-6

Second edition 2019. Northern Bee Books
Volume 1 ISBN 978-1-912271-42-9
Volume 2 ISBN 978-1-912271-43-6

Artwork DM Design and Print

Melinda's Bee-Hive

Contents:

EPISODE 1
BACKGROUND

Worker bees are the most numerous of the three types of bee in the hive, which are: the queen bee, the drone bee and the worker bee. This episode tells the story of the development of a worker bee, called Melinda, and she will take twenty-one days to develop from an egg, into a grub and finally, spins a cocoon in which to metamorphose or transform into a small adult bee.

Once the egg is deposited in its cell by the queen, it takes three days for it to grow into a grub with a tiny black head. 'Nurse' worker bees feed them a mixture of royal jelly and pollen in its cell. The 'Nurse' bees then cover the cell with wax. After metamorphosis is complete, the emerging bee will eat up the wax covering of its cell. Once out of the cell, it takes a while for the veins and arteries in its wings to fill up with hemolymph or 'bee blood'.

Worker bees fix broken bits of honeycomb and construct new cells all with wax they produce from glands in their vodies. Worker bees also feed the drones and attend to and feed the queen. They clear out any dead bees and guard at the entrance against intruders, like wasps. An essential part of the worker bee's jobs is to wet its belly fur from a source of water and bring it into the hive. The water is used to decrystalise honey, that is honey that has gone too hard to eat. They use honey to eat during bad weather and over the winter months.

Outside the hive, the workers finally become 'foraging' bees and fly to and fro from the hive collecting pollen and nectar to store in cells. There are some dangers for the foragers outside the hive like: rain, high winds, birds and other insects that like to eat them. Not all the foragers may make it back to their hive with their precious cargo of pollen and nectar. However, there are so many foragers in each hive that there will always be food coming in to be stored for the developing brood (the grubs) and for the other bees that stay in the hive like, the drones and other worker bees, as long as there are plenty of wild flowers growing in the fields, hedges and woodlands.

A First Adventure for Melinda, the honey bee

Hi! I'm Melinda, a new-born female honey bee

I live with all my family in a bee-hive, you see

I do all my queen tells me, it's never a chore

But flying's my passion and I'd like to do more

If she says, "Clean!", I clean up all day

And in the clean cells, new eggs she will lay

I polish many cells till brightly they shine

Feed grubs royal jelly, the pleasure's all mine!

While we're making new honeycomb and fixing the cracks

The Foragers all exercise the wings on their backs

The drones need some food, the queen needs attending

I'll guard at the entrance till this day is ending

The foragers are out flying high on the breeze

With collecting in mind they'll do it with ease

They're foraging from Daisies and Dandelions too

They'll gather yellow pollen, from Poppies it's blue

The sunflowers' heads track the sun's yellow light

Their pollen bags are full and day's end is in sight

Already it's dusk and they've done enough collecting

Up in the sky, there are thunder clouds gathering

It's raining! Drip! Drop! And they're in great trouble

The thunder is nearing and it's starting to rumble

Oh! no. They can't fly in the rain, they'll get so very wet

They'll hide in bluebells, no a foxglove's a safe bet

Saffron, the bumble bee, has had the same idea

So they share till the storm's gone and the sky's again clear

While the rain is falling and the thunder rolls

They stay calm and safe in their hidey-holes

When the sun reappears it's low in the sky

So the bees journey home to the warmth and the dry

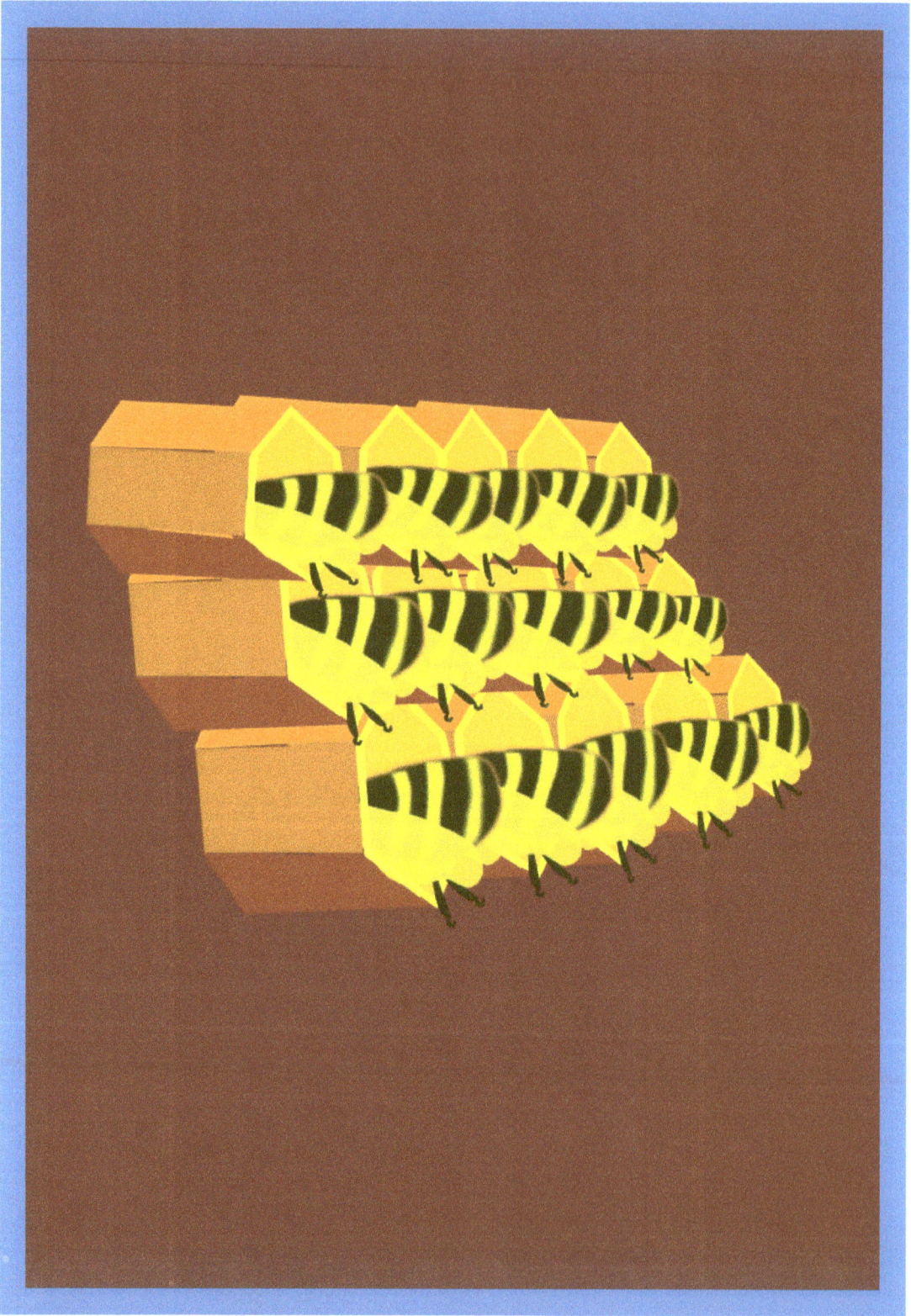

The Foragers return exhausted by their trip

Store away their pollen and drink nectar sip by sip

When the chores are all done and everyone's fed

And everything's quiet, I'll pick a cell for my bed.

All's well in the land of honey.

BZZZzzzz!

Remember! Melinda and her friends don't like to be touched.

They will sting you if you get to close.

EPISODE 2
BACKGROUND

Young honey bees begin by flexing their wing muscles on their backs and practise flying round the hive, building up their strength before they fly sometimes for many miles (or kilometres) on their foraging missions. Foraging bees start flying out from the hive on day twenty-two of their short lives. They seem to take off backwards and then circle the bee-hive a few times before leaving in the direction of the flowers. It is thought that they are making a mental map of the hive and surrounding plants and grasses so that they will be able to fly back to the correct hive.

Melinda takes to the skies

When Melinda awoke the sun was shining bright

"Right", said the queen, "let's get ready for your flight"

Melinda stood up straight and her wings she flexed

The muscles were stronger, she was ready for what came next

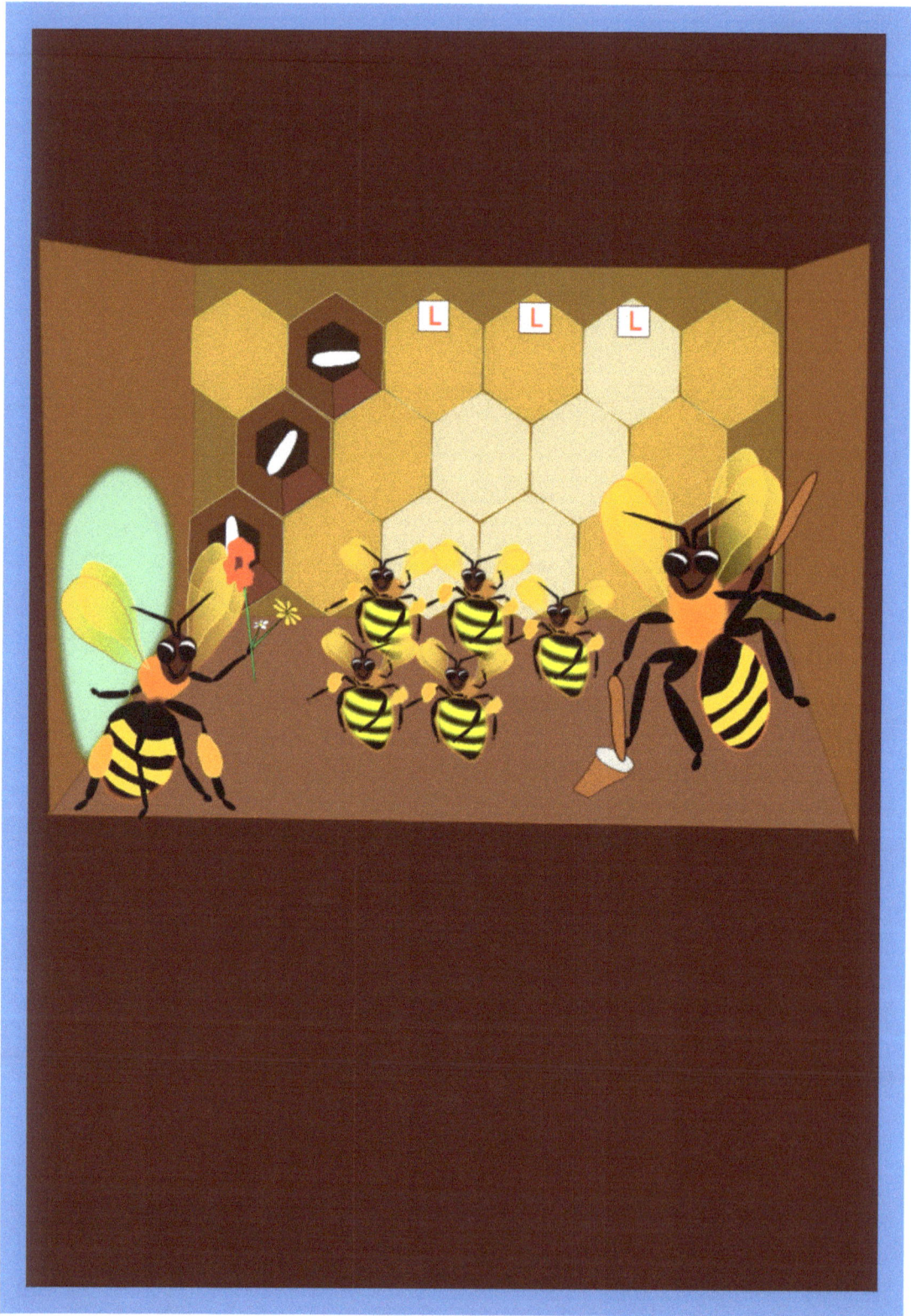

The flowers seemed to be calling them, Daisy was dancing, too

And so the team got ready, their first flying lesson to do

The drone was in charge and he drummed a rhythm out on the floor

And said, "Practice with your wings as you advance towards the door

Now, inside it is dark but outside it's very bright

And they blinked their big eyes in the morning sunlight

The drone pushed the last one out on to the landing strip

And under his guidance, they began to plan in earnest their trip

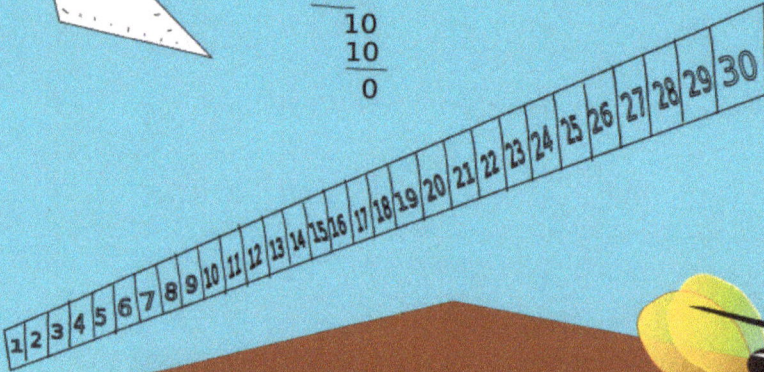

It involved some mathematics, geometry and long division

Calculating angles had to be made with precision

Flying wasn't so much fun now, it seemed at first very hard

But then, with practice, they wrote the principles down on a card

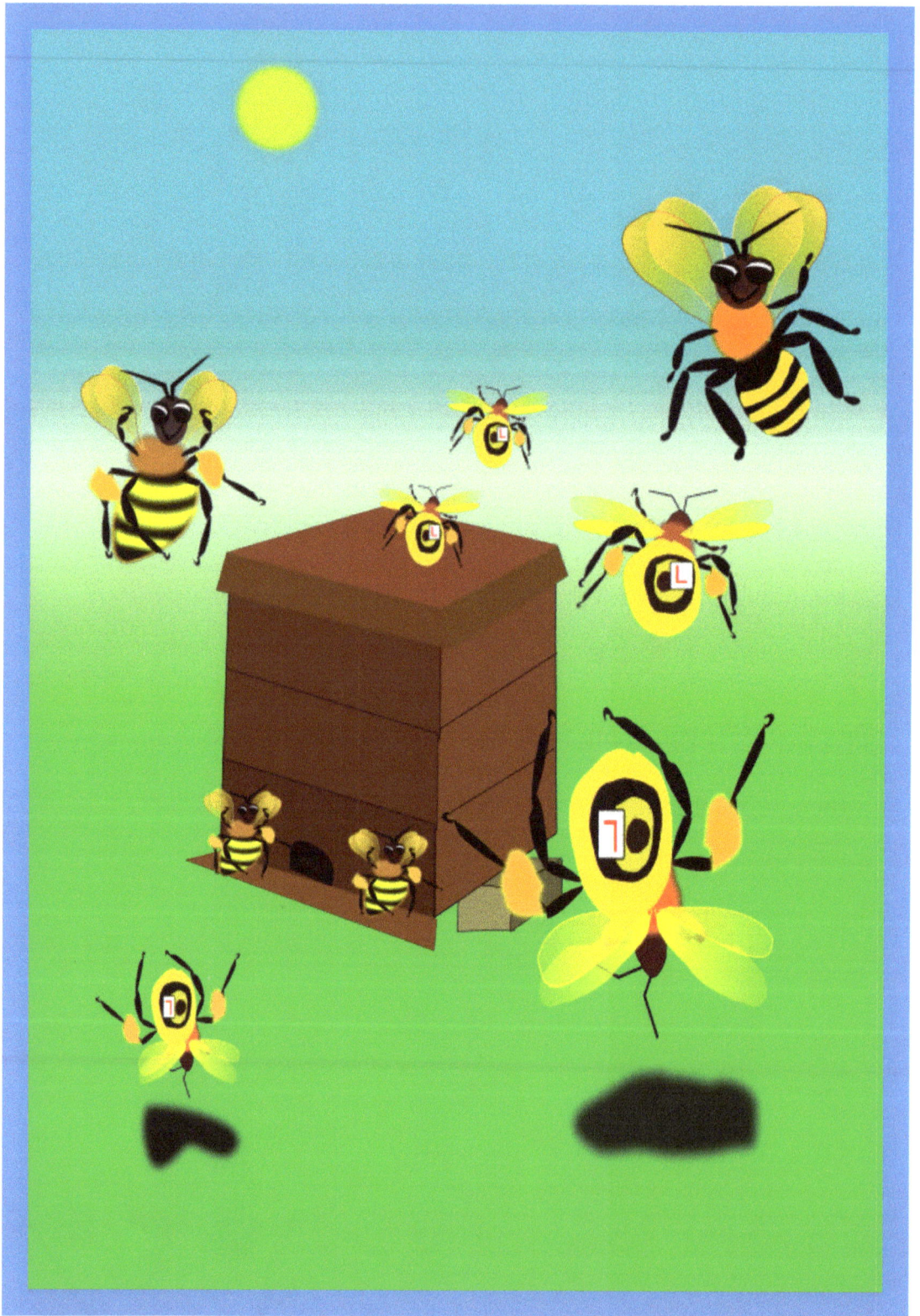

The first to lift off was Honeysuckle who landed on the roof

Closely followed by Ivy who landed back down with an "Ouf!"

Melinda's instructor was handsome and very kind

But reverse gear seemed at first, impossible to find

She reversed her wing beat and off backwards she shot

She looked at her hive so, in future, she'd know the spot

But a sudden gust of wind tipped her over and while

She tried to get balanced, she landed in a pile

She got up, dusted herself off and then tried anew

This time she went hurtling forwards, already black and blue

The instructor called out to her "Right wheel, please"

Melinda couldn't hear him and she hit the corner at speed

She bounced on the ground again and gritting her teeth

She'd do it the third time, she'd rise like a phoenix up from beneath

With vertical take-off perfected at last

She cornered superbly, she'd stuck to the task

Dipping her wings, she went left and right

And pictured herself going far into the night

The instructor, however, called for her to return

At the graduation ceremony she was about to earn...

Her 'WINGS' at last, well that was a surprise!

Now pollen and nectar would be her first prize.

All's well in the land of honey

BZZZzzzz!

Remember! Melinda and her friends don't like to be touched.

They will sting you if you get too close.

EPISODE 3
BACKGROUND

The scout bee's task is to travel away from the hive to find a good supply of pollen and nectar. She brings back a taster of this nectar and pollen and she gives it out to the other foraging bees whilst performing a dance where she indicates the location and distance of the flowers. The flowers can be up to three miles or more away from the hive. In this episode, the foragers are visiting some daffodils which are one of the first flowers to bloom in the spring each year. (N.B. The old varieties of daffodils have more nectar than the modern hybridised varieties that are popular these days). Honey bees are excellent pollinators. When they crawl past the flowers' anthers some pollen balls catch on their hairy bodies. As they crawl into another flower bell on their quest for nectar, some pollen balls stick to that flower's stigma and this is how the honey bees ensure that the flowers germinate new seeds or bulbs which will produce new flowers for the following year.

Honey bees also collect pollen from the tops of the six stamens which they put in the sacks on their legs. The bees find the most direct way to fly to their patch of flowers and back to the hive. In towns they encounter dangers. If they happen to fly through an open window then they will get trapped by the glass on the other side of the house. It just takes a few moments to catch the bee in a glass and slide a piece of paper or card underneath it. Then the glass can be turned the right way up and transported to the garden where the bee can safely be released. She will continue on her way back to her hive.

Melinda's pollen-collecting mission

Daisy, the scout, came in dancing, a-wagging her tail

She'd found flowers a-plenty and that was her tale

She'd flown really far and from the flowers she'd selected

She wanted to share all the pollen she'd collected

Now where's a secret, not even beekeepers know

Her dance shows the direction for the bees to follow

Already they're flying, out on the warm breeze

Will they find her flowers? Of course! They're bees

Along by the waterway and bobbed by the trees

They flew in formation, their treasure to seize

Daffodils! In clumps, their flower heads were fluttering

"There's nectar for all!" They seemed to be trumpeting

I'll take this one, said Melinda, the first to alight

She crawled up the flower head but try as she might

She couldn't stop the pollen from sticking to her hair

As she brushed past six stamens at the entrance to the lair

She sucked up sweet nectar she found in the gloom

She couldn't turn round for there wasn't much room

Backwards she'd crawl into the sunlight

Where she'd lick her lips with such delight

In each flower to follow when she crawled past

The pollen from her hairs to the stigma stuck fast

In this way, pollination of the flowers was completed

And she'd sucked up the nectar to which she'd been treated

Her pollen sacks, by now, had become quite heavy

And the nectar she'd drunk had a fragrance that was heady

She'd fly home directly, her pollen sacks to unload

And tell those there waiting, a story so bold...

She came back by the town and through an open window she flew

And buzzed round the house, up and down, enjoying the view

But behind the glass pane which reflected sun and sky

Which had made her a prisoner, just like Angus, the fly

They buzzed up and down and became very distraught

They skated on the glass behind which they were caught

They buzzed up and down more, it was making them late

And though they implored it, it would not let them escape

A glass jar came down on them, with a Clink! they were trapped

A card slid under them, and with their energy sapped...

They travelled in comfort, transported from inside

And released from their prison in the garden outside

Melinda came home tired, she'd made it at last

The queen would be pleased, it had been a blast!

Now Melinda was sleepy, her eyes were almost closed

Her wings were all crumpled, her heavy sacks yet to unload

She crawled into a cell and laid down her head

Too late to tell her story, they were all tucked up in bed.

All's well in the land of honey.

BZZZzzzz!

Remember! Melinda and her friends don't like to be touched.

They will sting you if you get too close.

EPISODE 4
BACKGROUND

As the summer months are ending, some beekeepers transport their hives to areas where plenty of the last of the flowers of the year are still blooming. There the bees can increase their supplies of pollen and nectar which they make into honey to eat through the winter months. The queen bee lays fewer eggs at this time of year as it would be hard to feed a full hive of bees now when there are few remaining flowers available for pollen and nectar collection. The beekeepers still have to check the eggs that are being laid and also to keep an eye on the bees' stores of honey. The transportation of the hive takes place in the evening when all the bees have returned for the night. However, some bees may be late in returning to the hive and are left behind to fend for themselves. (Bees from one hive can be introduced to another hive successfully without the guard bees killing many of them depending on whether the scent they give off is acceptable or not). As honeybees can fly from 3 to 7 miles from their hive on their foraging trips, the hive is re-located a long distance away in a new pollen and nectar-rich area. In this way, the honey bees do not get confused and try to fly home to their previous location as they will not be flying over territory that they will remember. It will all be new to them and they will make a new mind map of the area.

Melinda goes on holiday

Packing for Dover! We're going post-hast

At last to the coast, which is a nice place

"We'll frolic there on warm winds," we say

And visit scented flowers by the sea every day

We'll take good care of our little nation

But we won't let work spoil this very vacation

And as the sun sets itself down in the west

It's "Hello!" to the moon. The midgies are a pest!

The first day over, we'll sleep until it's late

We don't have to worry, we have no pressing date

Our queen's still laying eggs of which drones there aren't any

For winter's nearly here and we don't need so many

We wake up the next day and yawn

We won't tarry, it's already dawn

Strange flowers await our investigation in pairs

The nectar to extract, pollen collects on our hairs

The flowers are wild, it's a miracle they're still there

It's so enjoyable out and about, we haven't a care

The beekeepers come to see what eggs have been laid

They'll also check our health and what honey's been made

We make honey, that's our task

To feed our brood and others who ask!

Now the new queen is making a perfume so rare

It's causing us all to behave without care

Oh no, what's that stuff, cough, cough, on our chests?

It smells like you get from inside the wasps' nests

Wafting through the hive with increasing intensity

Making us all calm with its soothing quality

The Beekeeper looks at each honeycomb in turn

Through his clothes, we attack him with stings that burn

"We don't like losing the honey", to him we implore

We'll have to replace it now, that's going to be a chore

But as soon as he's gone, we're off again out

To Sea Heather and Gorse that is all about

From these flowers our aim is pollen and nectar collection

We'll make more honey and put it under our protection

On our return what a fright we all get

Where has the hive gone? It was here when we left!

We must work together to find our own patch of clover

We know that our GPS won't reach home from Dover.

Another hive? Yes, that's it, we'll try to join there

And in our endeavour, we'll just take great care

We notice a difference in communal whiff

But we've lost ours due to the puffer's niff

And so we're accepted within with provision

Our load of pollen's bound to sway their decision

They cordially invite us all to come inside

Where we feel protected, this is now our new hive.

All's well in the land of honey.

BZZZzzzz!

Remember! Melinda and her friends don't like to be touched.

They will sting you if you get too close.

Melinda, the honey bee

Max, the Hover fly

A honey bee visits some poppies

Saffron, the Bumble-bee

Wiley, the Wasp

Bees in a hive

WORKER

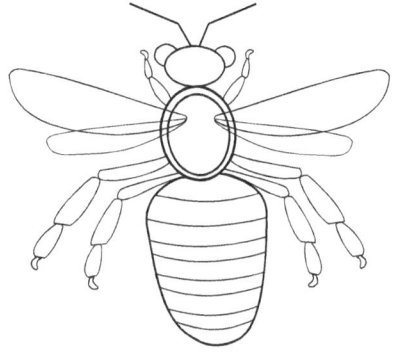

DRONE

QUEEN

Activities for creative minds

Drama
You could act out the story with your friends.

Modelling
You could make models of Melinda and her friends out of modelling clay or salt dough and paint them.

Mobile
You could cut out the outline graphics or trace them onto a separate sheet of paper, colour them in with bright colours and create a mobile.

Painting
You could paint a picture taken from an episode.

Storyline
You could create a new story or carry on from where these episodes finish off. What happened next...?